Nubiana

A True Story About A Very Special Kitty

Kristen Calenda

Published and Distributed by:
Angelnook Publishing, Inc.
1277 Cranston Street
Cranston, RI 02920
www.angelnookpublishing.com

ISBN-10: 1478341351
ISBN-13: 978-1478341352

Acknowledgments

(Listed in order of the fruition of this book. All services from friends were provided from the goodness of their hearts.)

All That Matters, Holistic and Yoga Center, for offering all the wonderful classes.

Foster Perry, for his inspirational "storytelling" lecture one Friday evening in August 2011, leading me to another (unplanned) class the following morning.

Kristos Tsompanelis, for teaching a seminar in the hermetic path (the Tree of Life), and for "lighting the fire," giving me the push I needed to start writing about Nubiana. Without his candor and zest, I am pretty sure the book would not have happened.

E.J. Finocchio, DVM, president, RISPCA, for his honesty and constructive criticism: helping me to create the best story about Nubiana.

Larry Snyder, my unconditional loving friend, for all the countless hours he spent proofreading and researching. His valuable opinions, keen insight, and artistic contributions were instrumental in the development of this book.

Stacey Richard, my dear sister, for typing my original handwritten draft into a Word document. (When you type with two fingers, this is huge!)

Diane Bilodeau, longtime friend, for loving Nubiana so much and for voicing her opinion about my original ending, prompting me to change it for the betterment of the book.

Luigia Soldà, children's librarian and very dear friend, for the hours spent helping me with sentence structure and for my first real lesson in computer navigation. She advised me a change to the original title.

Kelly Martin, my friend and children's author, for suggesting chapters for the book as well as a change to the original title. That makes two opinions that matter (Ouch!).

Robin Shippee and Doggie Do Pet Grooming, for allowing me to photograph the salon.

Eileen Watson, my neighbor, good friend, and godmother of my kids, for her assistance with the artwork critiquing.

Lori Hazard, for her help in editing and for providing me with thought-provoking suggestions.

Robert Bergantine, "the guru of the computer," for designing my beautiful web page, for his tech support, and for scanning photographs for this project.

Karen Daley, nurse and animal communicator, for her invaluable messages about Nubiana.

Danika Wayss, my young friend, neighbor, and inspirational artist, for the color/art design of the map insertion.

Mark Corvus, a new friend, for critiquing and editing the story toward the final stage.

Vicki Beliveau, my cousin, for offering to do the final edit before publication.

Pat Hastings for her support.

Chapter 1: Nubiana's Arrival

It was not too cold outside for a late January day in New England. Tony came home at four o'clock on Saturday afternoon. As he pulled his red truck into the driveway, his wife, Kristen, greeted him from the doorway.

Upon opening the tailgate of his pickup truck, she heard Tony say "Uh-oh." In the truck, Kristen spotted a gray crate. Inside the crate was a small, black cat.

"What's this all about?" demanded Kristen, standing with her hands on her hips.

Tony replied, "My friend Becky brought home this stray cat and named her Nubiana. She didn't know her roommate was allergic to cats, and was told she couldn't keep her. No one wants her for a pet. Becky asked me to take Nubiana to the animal shelter; she just couldn't bear to do it. I guess I got busy doing errands, and forgot," Tony explained.

"Well, it's too late to take her to the shelter now," Kristen angrily replied. "They're closed, so I guess we're stuck with her for the weekend."

Kristen didn't like cats very much, and Tony was well aware of that. Tony took Nubiana out of the crate and set her down on the back edge of the truck. She was very small for an adult cat. Her fur was dirty and matted together in knots.

"Put her in the garage," Kristen yelled. "She's not coming in the house like that!"

Word of Nubiana's arrival spread up and down the street. Curious neighbors came to greet her and brought her cat food to eat. Tony fetched a bowl of water for her to drink. All the neighbors petted Nubiana and held her in their arms.

"How can you touch her?" Kristen shouted. "She's filthy!"

Needless to say, Nubiana slept in the garage that night. Tony left the light on for her. He placed an old white bath towel inside the crate to make a soft bed for her to sleep on. As the sun began to set, Tony closed the garage door and he and Kristen went into the house for the rest of the night.

The next day was Sunday. It was sunny outside. The garage door stayed open all day. Nubiana explored the garden to go to the bathroom, but she stayed close by. Eileen, Kristen and Tony's next-door neighbor, stopped over to visit Nubiana again.

"I told my mother about the cat," Eileen stated. "She is willing to keep her, but

Nubiana has to be up-to-date with her shots. She also needs her fur shaved off to remove all the matted knots, and that will cost a lot. My mother doesn't have the extra money to pay for those things to be done."

Kristen and Tony did not want to see Nubiana go to an animal shelter. They agreed to take Nubiana to be cleaned up and shaved at the pet salon, and also to pay for her shots.

It was going to be very cold later that night. Kristen decided to let Nubiana into the house, but she would have to sleep in the basement in the laundry room. Tony put Nubiana into the crate and took her downstairs. Kristen followed, carrying Nubiana's food and water. As Nubiana looked around her new room, Kristen and Tony stood watch over her.

"She's funny looking. She looks like she only has one eye," Kristen said.

"No, she's got two eyes. You just can't see one of them very well," replied Tony. Nubiana spent the night alone again, behind a closed door.

Chapter 2: Spa Day at the Pet Salon

Monday morning came soon enough. Kristen contacted Robin, the groomer, at the pet salon. Robin agreed to shave Nubiana, but only after she got her shots at the doctor's office. Every animal hospital that Kristen telephoned charged one hundred dollars for two shots.

"There's no way I'm spending one hundred dollars on a cat!" Kristen yelled after hanging up the phone. It was her third call that morning.

The next phone call was her lucky one. The Rhode Island Society for the Prevention of Cruelty to Animals (called the RISPCA, for short) said it would provide two shots for Nubiana for only twenty dollars. Kristen put Nubiana into the crate, and then carried her to the car. Off they drove to the RISPCA. When they arrived, a young girl showed Kristen how to clean Nubiana's nose and eyes. They were both full of crusty mucus.

The doctor came into the room and took Nubiana to give her a quick checkup. After he gave Nubiana her shots, he handed Kristen a small bottle of medicine to take home. Kristen wasn't sure what it was for, but didn't bother to ask. She was halfway to getting rid of Nubiana. Kristen put Nubiana back into the car and off to the pet salon they went.

Upon their arrival at the pet salon, Robin came out of the back room to greet them. She took a long look at Nubiana. "This could take a while," is all she said.

"No problem," said Kristen. "I have to go to the bank. See you in an hour." She knew she was leaving Nubiana in good hands.

When Kristen returned, Nubiana was in a big bathtub, standing on her back legs. Her front paws were hanging onto the edge of the tub. She was soaking wet and shaved down to her skin! Nubiana's eyes opened wide at the sight of Kristen.

"Wow!" Kristen blurted out. "She's so tiny!"

Robin held up a piece of fur. It was from one side of Nubiana's body. It looked like a little rug.

"See this piece?" Robin pointed to a small flap of fur dangling from one end. "This is her ear fur. It was stuck to her shoulder." Robin bent her own head to one side, trying to touch her shoulder with her ear. "It was causing Nubiana's head to be crooked; bent to one side!" cried Robin. "Stuck like that all the time!"

"That's why it looked like Nubiana only had one eye!" exclaimed Kristen.

And what beautiful eyes she had! They were big, golden yellow, round eyes, just like the sun. She had a little pink tongue that hung out of her mouth, off to one side.

Nubiana was now a light gray color where her fur had been shaved. Her head was black and so was the tip of her tail where her black fur remained unshaved. It looked just like an artist's paintbrush! She wore four little black boots of fur on her feet. Robin called this hairdo "the lion cut." And that's just what Nubiana looked like – a lion cub.

Nubiana was a Persian cat. Her face was as flat as a pancake. Her nose was flat too, with two tiny holes for her to breathe from. That cute little nose sat high, almost between her eyes. Oh, those eyes! How they just made you melt like ice cream. How beautiful she was!

Robin took Nubiana out of the tub and placed her on the worktable. Her nails needed cutting next. "I can't promise I won't hurt her," Robin told Kristen. "Nubiana's nails have grown so long that they have curled right back into the bottom of her feet!"

Robin explained to Kristen that was how a cat's nails grew – curled. It was up to the animal's guardian to see that they were trimmed every so often. If not, this is what could happen. She also advised Kristen to brush Nubiana at least once a week, once her fur grew back. This would keep her fur from becoming tangled and matted again.

"Do what you need to do," Kristen said.

One by one, she watched Robin cut Nubiana's nails. Nubiana never cried or tried to get away. She was such a good kitty. When Robin was finished, Nubiana had tiny holes in the bottom of her feet where the nails had grown. Kristen realized this was what the medicine was for; it was to help heal Nubiana's wounds. Kristen would have to apply the medicine to Nubiana's paws for a few days. Robin told her that Nubiana was in a lot of pain before arriving at the salon. She was sure that she was a much happier kitty now. They agreed that "a groomed kitty makes for a happy and healthy kitty." Kristen paid Robin for her services and thanked her. She put Nubiana back into the crate and out of the salon they went.

Chapter 3: A New Home

When they arrived home, Nubiana was allowed to walk through the house. As she explored, Kristen telephoned Eileen.

"We're home now, and Nubiana is all cleaned up."

"I'll be right over to get her," Eileen said.

"Not just yet – she needs medicine for a few days," replied Kristen.

"My mother has had pets her whole life; she can do it," said Eileen.

"No. I want to finish what I started," Kristen said.

"You're going to end up keeping that cat!" joked Eileen.

And she was right! The neighbors teased Kristen and Tony about deciding to keep Nubiana. Kristen had always made it known to everyone that she didn't like cats – AT ALL! Nubiana weighed only six pounds, which was not a lot for an adult cat. Her body was not much bigger than a loaf of bread. She never meowed. It was like she had no voice. Her little pink tongue always hung out of her mouth, off to one side. Her face was so sweet; she almost looked like a little doll.

The first special gift Kristen wanted to buy for Nubiana was a collar. She went back to see Robin at the pet salon. Kristen chose a deep rose cloth collar, decorated with tiny pale pink flowers. A raspberry-colored nametag was selected next. Robin advised Kristen to have two telephone numbers printed on the back, along with the cat's name. If Nubiana were to ever get lost, hopefully someone would find her and call Tony or Kristen. They all wanted Nubiana to always be safe.

It didn't take long for Kristen and Tony to fall in love with Nubiana. Every night she would sleep on Tony's pillow, just above his head. She would sit with Kristen in the big lounging chair while she read books or watched TV. With a jingle of the bell on her collar, she faithfully came to greet them at the door when they arrived home. Nubiana was the perfect housemate.

A little later that winter, Kristen took Nubiana to the animal hospital for a full checkup and tests. Dr. Korry was the owner of the hospital. She pointed out that two of Nubiana's teeth were infected and should be removed. This would allow Nubiana to eat her food without any pain. Kristen's wallet was in a lot of pain too! It cost over five hundred dollars to have Nubiana's dental work done. But Nubiana was worth it. She had already won over Kristen and Tony's hearts and was now a member of the family.

By the time spring arrived, Nubiana was being referred to as "Nubes." Tony liked to call her "Baby Nubes." Kristen's favorite nickname for her was "Nubi-Nu." Her black fur was beginning to grow back. Nubiana was an indoor cat, but she got to go outside into the garden and pose for pictures. She tiptoed among the giant red tulips and sniffed the purple pansies. The sunshine kissed her face as she listened to the chirping birds.

Nubiana was not allowed to go outside by herself, to keep her safe from large birds and animals. Stray cats and dogs could hurt her in a fight. Hawks and owls could swoop down and carry her away in their claws for a tasty meal. Foxes and coyotes could easily grasp her in their jaws for a yummy dinner. While Kristen was out working in the garden, Nubiana would often join her. Kristen would keep Nubiana safe by placing her in a harness and would tie her leash to a chair. Nubes would soak up the sunshine while lying on the patio furniture in a big, soft cat bed. She was Kristen's little princess.

Nubiana was very spoiled. She got to go everywhere with Kristen and Tony. While traveling in the car, Nubes wore a special harness around her body. This allowed her to be secured in the seat with the seat belt, just like Kristen and Tony. If an accident were to happen, the seat belt would keep her from being thrown about the inside of the car, or worse, thrown out the window. There were times when traveling in the car that Nubiana was placed inside her crate instead. The crate was always seat-belted too, keeping Nubiana safe in the car at all times.

Chapter 4: Summer Fun

Tony and Kristen were good friends with Captain Jon and his wife Christine. They had a huge, beautiful boat and kept it at a marina near Tony and Kristen's home. Captain Jon and Christine lived far away in New Hampshire. They did not always have time to travel to Rhode Island to spend the weekend on their boat. They let Nubiana, Kristen and Tony sleep on board the boat whenever they wanted, all summer long. The boat had lots of huge windows. Nubes liked to sit up high at the helm and watch all the boats sail by in the bay.

Nubiana was the star on the docks at the marina, and everybody loved her. In the afternoon the bands would play music. When the dancing began, Nubes joined in the fun. Tony would place Nubiana on the table when he and Kristen enjoyed their meal outdoors at the restaurant. She was so sweet and friendly; Nubes would let anybody hold her. She was one of a kind.

Kristen and Nubes would take many walks together along the water's edge. Nubiana would be in a small cloth bag, hanging from Kristen's shoulder. Her little head always poked out. She did not want to miss a thing! Every so often, someone passing by would stop and ask to meet her. Nubiana was Kristen's pride and joy. She showed her off to everyone they met.

Summertime brought the three to Plymouth, Massachusetts. There, they saw Plymouth Rock. This is where the Pilgrims landed when arriving in America. As you can imagine, Nubiana was a bigger attraction than the rock! People remarked how unusual it was to see a cat in public, in a tote bag, and not trying to get away!

Nubes was even allowed to sleep in the motel. She had her own playpen to sleep in, just like a baby. It had a fishnet cover to keep her safe inside when Kristen and Tony went out alone. She was always very good, very quiet. The highlight of the Plymouth trip was when Nubiana went on a whale watch tour on the ocean! Her eyes grew huge when she saw the whales. "They're too big for me to catch!" she surely must have been thinking. There were a lot of children on the trip too. They each took a turn petting Nubiana's head. She even wore her life vest for the boat trip; it was a bright, sunny yellow, just like her eyes.

Chapter 5: A Busy Autumn

When summer turned to fall, Nubes got to go camping. Not in a tent, but in a big camper. Off to Lake George, New York, they went. Nubes liked to look out the windows. The trees were bright shades of red, yellow and orange. Through the mountains they climbed until reaching the campground in the woods. At night, they all sat by the campfire Tony made. Nubiana loved to watch the flames flicker as she snuggled in Tony's arms. She could feel the fire warm her body on the cool autumn night.

The next day they took their car onto a special ferry. Across Lake Champlain they traveled to another state, Vermont. Vermont had rolling farmlands nestled in the mountains. Early fall foliage bordered green fields. Red barns dotted the fields along with shiny silver silos that contained the farm animals' food. Nubiana was enjoying the view.

The car ride ended in a charming town. There was a sparkling river that ran through the village, scattering waterfalls among the old buildings. Houses and shops boasted window boxes filled with brightly colored fall flowers. Nubes got to eat lunch at an outdoor café. As people passed by, they would stop to pet Nubiana. All remarked on what a good kitty she was.

Returning to Lake George, they spent another day strolling through a beautiful park and lots of shops. Nubiana had her very own pet stroller, which was bright orange. It had a black screen door in the front and a screen window in the back for her to look out of. There was even a screen window at the top to let the sunshine on her body. It was always nice to have Nubes in the stroller when it came time to cross the busy streets. Cars would stop to let "the lady with the baby stroller" cross safely. Kristen would always laugh when this happened. It was hard to see Nubiana through the black screen with her black fur. They were all having such a good time.

Once they were back at home in Rhode Island, Kristen realized how grateful she was to have Nubiana in her life. She wanted to thank the RISPCA for all its help. It was time to "give back." Kristen decided to participate in the annual RISPCA dog walk with Nubiana. They headed out together to visit their neighbors and friends and to ask for their support. The money that people donated would go to a good cause. Funds raised would help feed and care for all the homeless animals in the shelter until they could find a new home with a loving family.

It was very cold on the day of the dog walk event. Nubiana wore a pale pink coat with white fluffy trim. She was the only cat there. Kristen carried her in the tote bag, as they walked through the windy park with hundreds of dogs and their owners. This was a hard task for Kristen to do. When she was a young girl, a dog had bitten her on the leg, and she was still a little scared of dogs. She held on tight to Nubiana, and tried to think of all the homeless animals she was helping. These good thoughts gave her courage, helping Kristen toward her goal, and helping her have a good time as well with Nubes.

When the walk was over, prizes were given to the top three participants. Not to those who walked the fastest, but to those who had collected the most money for the animal shelter. Nubiana and Kristen received the second-place prize. They had collected two hundred eighty-three dollars! Nubes received a big basket full of treats and toys that were donated by local pet shops. What a rewarding day!

The end of October was approaching fast and so was Halloween. "What could Nubiana be?" wondered Kristen. With those big yellow eyes and black flat face, the best choice would be a sunflower, of course! Kristen made Nubes a one-of-a-kind bonnet. The bright yellow petals matched her eyes perfectly. They were made from a stiff felt fabric, allowing them to stand up around Nubiana's face. Kristen sewed seven large petals onto a strip of bright green soft felt that wrapped around Nubiana's head. Velcro was sewn to the ends, holding it in place. Satin orange pumpkins, the size of a dime, were sewn in between all the petals on the band. Nubiana looked wonderful! All the trick-or-treaters loved Nubiana's costume when knocking on their door on Halloween night. Nubiana, however, was not a happy camper. She couldn't wait for the silly thing to be off her head!

Chapter 6: A New Friend

In the beginning of December, Kristen and Tony decided to take a special trip to Nantucket Island in Massachusetts, but the hotel did not allow pets. Nubiana would have to stay home this time. She would be under Eileen's care.

Kristen and Tony were not gone very long before missing Nubiana. Tony was sad and feeling bad about leaving her home. He decided that Nubiana should have a friend. Tony was on the computer at the hotel, looking for a friend for Nubiana, when Kristen woke up that morning.

"Come see what I found," Tony said. There, on the computer screen, was a picture of a black cat with a flat face and big yellow eyes.

"That looks just like Nubiana!" Kristen blurted out.

His name is Oscar," Tony replied. "He lives in Connecticut. Oscar is living with a foster mom because there is no room at the shelter for him. Someone found him on the street eating out of trashcans!" They agreed that Oscar needed a good home and telephoned the rescue group right away.

Before the day was over, the animal rescue group contacted Dr. Korry. They needed to be sure Kristen and Tony would be good pet guardians. Dr. Korry assured them Oscar would be well taken care of. She also told them how much Kristen and Tony had already done for Nubiana in such a short time. It would take a few days before they would know if Oscar would be joining their family.

The trip was fun, but neither of them could stop thinking about Nubes. By the time they returned home four days later, Nubes was missing them just as much as they missed her. She gave Kristen and Tony kisses with her little pink tongue, all over their faces. What a treasure Nubiana was!

Kristen and Tony brought Eileen gifts they purchased on the island to thank her for taking care of Nubes. She had done such a good job, Kristen and Tony asked her if she would be Nubiana's "godmother." Much to their delight, she accepted gladly with a big "YES." She was now referred to as "Godmother Eileen."

A few days passed before Kristen and Tony received a call from the animal rescue group in Connecticut. Oscar was going to be their newest family member! It was one week to the day from when they had found Oscar on the Internet, and now Kristen and Tony were driving to Connecticut to pick him up. What a wonderful Christmas it was going to be!

Oscar loved Nubiana right away. Other than his plump body, the only way to tell them apart was by Nubiana's little pink tongue, hanging out from her mouth. Their fur was long and very fluffy. Small ears topped their heads while short legs kept their bellies close to the ground. They would lie together under the white Christmas tree while looking up at the hundreds of white twinkling lights for hours.

Kristen and Tony took their fine furry friends to the pet store to see Santa Claus. They all wore red stocking caps on their heads. The four posed with Santa Claus for their first Christmas photograph together. The money they paid to purchase the photos was going toward helping the animals at the shelter.

On Christmas morning, there were lots of gifts for Oscar and Nubes. New soft cat beds, mouse toys, new collars, and a big scratching post to climb. Nubes gave her usual kisses to Kristen and Tony. Oscar liked to give big hugs around their necks with his front paws. Oscar had two big white whiskers that curled toward the front of his face. His whiskers would tickle their faces and would make Tony and Kristen laugh.

The last week of January arrived. Nubiana had been with Kristen and Tony for one year already. How fast it had gone by! They loved her so much and were so happy they had found a friend for her. The four were delighted to have one another, and be a family.

Chapter 7: Spring Has Sprung

Kristen's birthday was at the end of March, and it was approaching fast. She wanted to celebrate it in an extra-special way. Tony found the perfect pet-friendly inn on the Internet, two and a half hours away in Massachusetts. Together they packed the car and the four of them headed east to Cape Cod.

The inn was located in Provincetown, at the tip of the Cape, which was bordered by the sea on both sides. Their room had a huge picture window that overlooked the park next door. Oscar's and Nubiana's eyes opened wide as they sat on the window ledge! Together they watched the squirrels and dogs play in the park, as the birds sang, perched in the newly budding trees. At night, they would cuddle together in front of the warm fireplace.

The innkeeper allowed her guests to bring their pets into the grand living room. It was filled with cozy sofas and chairs for the guests to enjoy tea and homemade cookies next to a crackling fire. As always, Oscar and Nubiana were the only cat guests. Dogs of various sizes relaxed in the room, including a really big poodle. Tony placed Oscar on the poodle's back for his very first piggyback ride! All the guests laughed at such a silly sight. What a wonderful birthday Kristen was having! It would be one that she would never forget.

As the weather warmed and April flowers began to bloom, it was time to start camping again. This time they all went to the seashore in southern Rhode Island to camp. This was right up Oscar's and Nubiana's alley – lying in the sun, walking on their leashes in the dunes, the sand between their toes, and lots of sea grass to explore in. The seagulls soared above as the warm wind blew across their faces. Tiny birds raced along the ocean's edge, which was shared by crabs and jellyfish. Everything was magical at the beach.

Early one morning in May, Kristen went downstairs to the kitchen from her bedroom. Oscar, as usual, was already waiting at the food station. As Kristen poured fresh food into their bowls, Nubiana joined Oscar to eat.

While the cats ate breakfast, Kristen went back upstairs to get ready for work. It was already hot outside. The air conditioner was running. She turned on the TV to watch the morning news. The air conditioner was loud. Kristen turned the TV volume higher so she could hear the show. She got dressed and made the bed.

Then Kristen heard a mourning dove singing. "Ooahoo oo oo oo." How she loved their song. It always made her stop wherever she was. "Ooahoo oo oo oo." Kristen turned to the window to look for the dove, but she realized it was closed because the air conditioner was on. The TV was loud! How could this be? The dove's singing was clear to her ear. Where was it coming from? "Ooahoo oo oo oo." Something wasn't right. She had to find the mourning dove.

Downstairs she went. As Kristen turned the corner, she saw Oscar. He was sitting on the carpet under a chair in the dining room. Next to him lay Nubiana. She seemed lifeless. Her eyes were open, but staring blankly into the air. Her little pink tongue hung out of her mouth. Kristen ran to them screaming "Nubiana!" As Kristen knelt down, Oscar lay down beside her. Scooping up Nubiana into her arms, she cried her little kitty's name over and over.

"Nubiana, Nubiana, Nubiana!" The tears streamed down her face. "Please Nubiana, don't leave me!" Kristen sobbed. "No, no, don't leave me!"

It was Nubiana's time to cross over the rainbow bridge that morning. She was not alone. Oscar was with her and so were the angels. Kristen was sure it was indeed the angels who sent the song of the mourning dove to her. She was grateful for their gift, so she too could be with Nubiana. As her tears continued to flow down her cheeks, falling onto Nubiana's face, Kristen rocked Nubiana in her arms, as she took her last breath.

Chapter 8: A Heart Heals

Kristen and Tony remained sad and cried for many, many days. Nubiana was always on their minds. They missed having Nubiana greet them at the door; the jingle of her collar bell rang no more. Oscar was always ready with big hugs to help ease their pain.

To help mend her broken heart, Kristen decided to clear out an overgrown garden at the entry to her home. Oscar watched through the glass door as she planted yellow tulips and golden daffodils that spring to remind her of Nubiana's eyes. Deep pink roses and pale pink lilies were added to represent Nubiana's tongue. Kristen placed yellow and white pansies under a metal birdbath. Three tiny metal birds decorated the edge. Tony hung a bird feeder from the perch of a copper birdhouse that sat high above the garden on a pole. They knew that bird watching was one of Nubiana's favorite things to do. A cement statue of a Persian cat peeked through some English ivy. At the edge of the garden near the door, Kristen placed an engraved stepping-stone. It read:

Nubiana: prettiest Persian princess.
Went boating, camping and fine dining.

Every day when leaving or entering their home, Kristen always had a smile on her face when walking past the garden. Fond thoughts of her little friend and the happy times they shared gave her a sense of peace. The love Nubiana had brought to Kristen would always stay with her, close to her heart. As the days turned to weeks and then to months, Kristen and Tony's sadness grew less and less.

A special place inside the family room was dedicated in honor of Nubiana. Pictures of Nubiana were displayed in pretty frames. A small colorful album was filled with more photos of Nubiana and many of their adventures together. It stood next to a small wooden box that held her pink collar and nametag. Proudly displayed in a clear glass jar was Nubiana's Halloween sunflower bonnet.

From time to time Kristen would poke through the pink glass box that held all the loving cards friends sent after Nubiana was gone. Sometimes, when she read them, tears filled her eyes, but they were always followed by a big smile. Joy filled her heart at the thought of just how much Nubiana was truly loved. She had touched not just Kristen and Tony's lives, but the lives of everyone who had the pleasure of meeting her.

Kristen knew she needed to put her thoughts and feelings about Nubiana on paper. She wrote a story about their short time together, expressing her love for her precious Nubi-Nu. Memories of the adventures they shared, and of all the places they traveled together, filled the pages effortlessly.

Inside the car's glove box, Kristen searched for a road map of New England. One by one, she circled each town she and Tony had visited with Baby Nubes. The last two towns circled were those where Oscar joined them too.

A bright yellow scrapbook was used to showcase the story inside. Kristen carefully glued the map onto one of the pages. Several of her favorite photos of Nubes were added to the book as well. On the cover, with a bright pink marker, she proudly wrote: NUBIANA: A TRUE STORY ABOUT A VERY SPECIAL KITTY.

Each spring, as new growth sprouted, Kristen would lovingly tend to her Nubiana Garden. While caring for the flowers, she would think about how she had cared for Nubiana. Throughout the seasons, she nurtured the flowers to their fullest blooms, just as Nubiana had nurtured her.

Years later, Tony and Kristen still missed Nubiana very much. After all, she was such a very special kitty – one in a million. It was during those years Kristen finally knew what fine gifts Nubiana had brought with her upon entering their lives. What Kristen had always thought to be just a happy accident she now knew was meant to be. Before Nubiana's arrival she didn't like cats AT ALL! Nubiana taught her love and respect, not just for cats, but also for all animals, great and small. Without Nubiana, Oscar would not be part of their lives, and now they loved him just as much. But mostly, she taught Kristen "not to judge a book by its cover, because you never know what you may find inside." She would always be thankful to Nubiana for this gift, and would always love her, and never forget her. Kristen was sure that Oscar and Nubiana were only the beginning of many more cats to come to bless her life and open her heart.

--Nubiana snuggling in her favorite cow blanket (2006)

--Nubiana at the helm of Captain Jon and Christine's 50-foot motor yacht (summer 2006)

--Nubiana's first photo in her new home, after being shaved down to her skin (January 2006)

--Nubiana basking in the sun on the chaise lounge (autumn 2006)

--Nubiana and Kristen boat lounging (summer 2006)

--Giant red lobster? No, it's Nubiana and Tony in Plymouth, Mass! (summer 2006)

--Nubiana and Tony in Plymouth, Mass.(summer 2006)

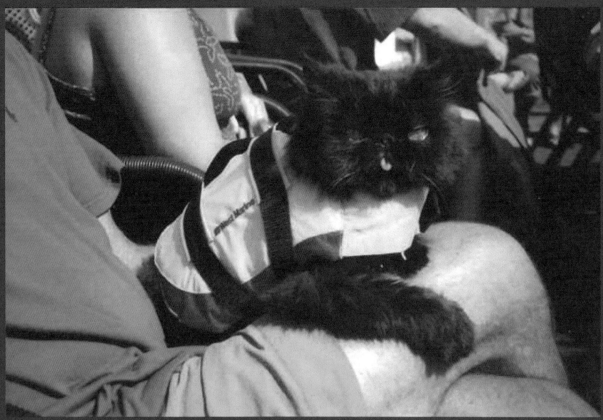

--Nubi-Nu sporting her life vest during the whale watch boat tour (summer 2006)

--The Fort Ticonderoga ferry that took Nubiana, Kristen and
Tony across the lake from New York to Vermont

--Second Place Winner! Kristen and Nubiana at the pet store for the Halloween costume contest and photo shoot (October 2006)

--Kristen and Nubiana cat napping (February 2006)

--Tony, Kristen and Nubiana at a different pet store for the Halloween costume contest, second place again! (October 2006)

--Nubiana modeling her sunflower
bonnet in Danika's yard (October 2006)

--Nubiana at the RISPCA dog walk
(October 2006)

--Nubiana tiptoeing among the
purple pansies (May 2006)

--Oscar and Kristen
(February 2012)

--Rainbow over East Matunuck
beach, RI (September 2011)

--Nubiana garden statues (April 2012)

--Oscar in the Nubiana garden sniffing flowers (April 2012)

--Kristen and Oscar enjoying the Nubiana garden (April 2012)

--Oscar lounging on the chaise at sunset (May 2012)

She was the teeny, tiny, baby Nubiana
She luuuuuuuvvved to give the kisses to the mama
But, sometimes.............................she just didn't wanna
Nubiana

Kristen, Tony, and Nubiana at the beach in Wakefield, RI (September 2006)

Thank you Ant, my wonderful husband of twenty years, for forgetting to take Nubiana to her intended destination. Thank you Nubiana for choosing to stay with us, and making me the better person I am today.

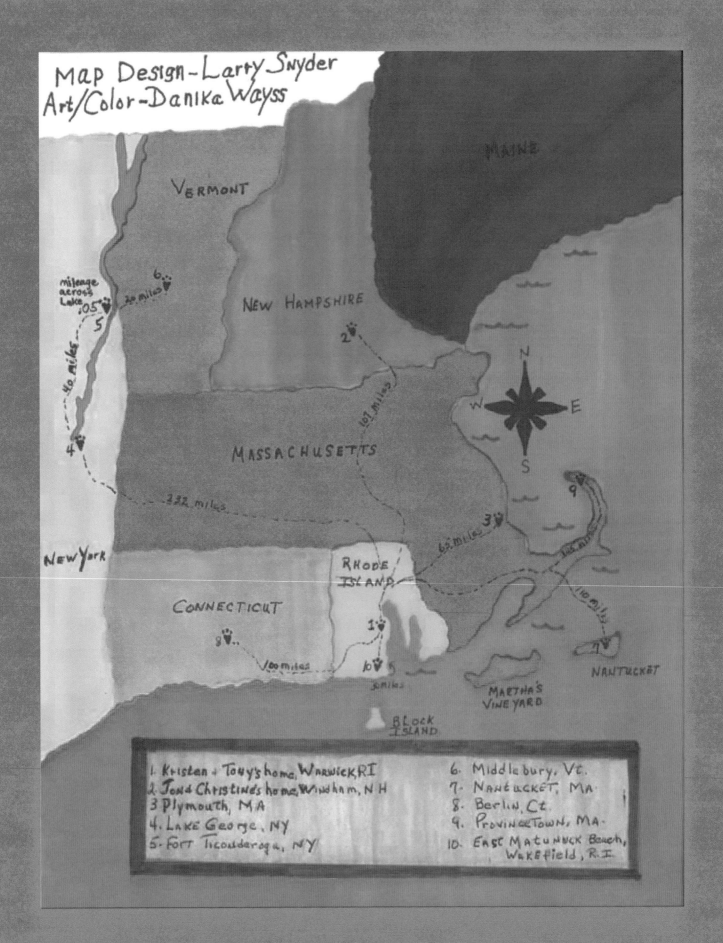

Map of New England

Oscar with his two new roommates, Gracie (left) and Junebug (May 2012)

Contacts

All That Matters, Holistic and Yoga Center, 315 Main St., Wakefield, RI 02879, (401) 782-2126, www.allthatmatters.com

Foster Perry, www.goldenhummingbird.com

Kristos Tsompanelis, www.kristosmusic.com

E.J. Finocchio, DVM, RISPCA, 186 Amaral St., Riverside, RI 02915, (401) 438-8150, www.RISPCA.com

Doggie Do Pet Grooming, 2190 Broad St., Cranston, RI 02905, (401) 941-3544

Laurie Hazard, Ed.D., Director of the Academic Center for Excellence, Bryant University, Smithfield, RI 02917, lhazard@bryant.edu

Rob Bergantine, Interopic Technology Consulting, 470 Washington St., Coventry, RI 02816, (401) 400-0033, www.Interopic.com

Karen Daley, Animal and Spirit Communication, Reiki Master, (508) 672-6710, animalandspirittalk.com

Pat Hastings, MS, LCDP, www.SimplyaWomanofFaith.com

Kristen Calenda, www.kristencalenda.com

Nubiana Calenda: visit on Facebook

Books can be purchased at www.bn.com, www.amazon.com, and
Positive New Beginnings, 877 Broadway, East Providence, RI 02914, (401) 432-7195